Joseph Shultz

Observations in the North-West

Containing an account of a trip to Alaska

Joseph Shultz

Observations in the North-West
Containing an account of a trip to Alaska

ISBN/EAN: 9783337147921

Printed in Europe, USA, Canada, Australia, Japan

Cover: Foto ©Andreas Hilbeck / pixelio.de

More available books at **www.hansebooks.com**

OBSERVATIONS

IN THE

NORTH-WEST,

CONTAINING AN

ACCOUNT OF A TRIP TO ALASKA, WHALE STORY, MOOSE STORY, DESCRIPTION OF RELICS IN SCIENCE AND ART GALLERIES, THE MINNEHAHA FALLS, MANNERS AND CUSTOMS OF THE PEOPLE, ETC.

BY

JOSEPH S. SHULTZ.

1892:
RECORD BOOK AND JOB OFFICE,
ADA, OHIO.

PREFACE.

The six main objects for the appearance of this small book are:

FIRST—To awaken the perceptive faculties.

SECOND—It will also be found beneficial in history, by associating the events and relics with the dates, thus making history real.

THIRD—Create an incentive for investigation.

FOURTH—To awaken interest in museums, science and art galleries.

FIFTH—To notice nature, human and Divine as well as changes in the social conditions.

SIXTH—As a supplementary reading book.

I conclude by wishing this geographical novel to be a true friend to all who read it, although it may chasten severely at times.

J. S. S.

FEDERAL BUILDING AT THE WORLD'S FAIR.

OBSERVATIONS
IN THE
NORTH-WEST.

A trip to the Northwest fills one with romantic experiences and arouses an interest in humanity. The sublime and beautiful as well as the ridiculous is presented on every hand. Here, especially in the land of the Dakotas, abide all races and classes, each alike in some respects but different in the main.

MANNERS AND CUSTOMS OF THE RUSSIANS.

About twenty years ago whole colonies came from the region of the Black Sea. Some settled in Manitoba, Canada, others in the Southwestern part of Minnesota, still a larger colony settled in the southeastern part of South Dakota, near Sioux Falls. A small settlement of fifteen families moved to the northwestern part of Iowa; large colonies are also in Northern Nebraska and Southern Kansas. One family is in Oregon.

As a rule these people are very economical, industrious and religious, living in one story houses made of unburnt brick with the stable and house adjoining. The roofs are of long wild grass. The dwellings of the Russians in Iowa are, however, similar to our American houses. In some localities German schools are held in the Winter and the pupils are instructed in reading, writing and Bible stories. The studies of temperance, hygiene and civil government in these schools are unknown but the English people make it compulsory.

A VISIT TO THEIR CHURCHES.

We see the Churches crowded, and services are held from 10 A. M. to 4 P. M., only stopping a short time at noon to attend to the horses. They bring a lunch with them which consists of a few dry crusts of bread and a bottle of coffee. The ladies and gentlemen do not sit together as is customary in more enlightened communities. No young man is allowed to escort a lady to or from Church unless engaged. The preaching is done by some good German farmer.

The Russians eat on an average four meals per day. Breakfast, consisting of four cups of coffee without cream or sugar, and a few dry biscuits without syrup or butter. For dinner the menu is coffee, rye bread and a large dishpan full of cabbage which stands in the center of the table, to which each person reaches forth and eats out of the bowl with a spoon. Seldom a plate is used and if a person should ask for a napkin he would be ostracized from society because they think it would be simply for style and displeasing in the sight of God. At 4 o'clock vesper is eaten which is similar to the breakfast. The fourth and main meal being at 9 o'clock, consisting of the usual drink, coffee, wheat or rye bread, beef or pork, and potatoes. On special occasions they have a dish made of prunes, raisins and spices boiled in milk. They also pickle whole water-melons which are eaten for a lunch before retiring. The seeds of sunflowers are eaten instead of pop corn, hickorynuts and apples.

All articles in and around the house are hand made. The bedsteads are merely a few boards nailed together, with hay instead of a mattress. This reminds me of a Russian's first experience in a hotel. After being assigned to his room, the night clerk told him to lock the door, or everything would be at his own risk; this seemed somewhat strange to the guest, but concluded to do as advised. So he hastened to bed for he had walked himself tired in visiting places of interest. But lo! just as he sat on the bed the springs compressed and he was lowered nearly a foot. This frightened him so that he jumped into the middle of the floor. He next lit the lamp and began to scrutinize the place very carefully but could not see a trap door. After an hour of meditation he concluded to let the light burn and get into bed easily, but sleep had passed from him and in the morning he demanded an explanation.

The Norwegians are a little more cultured and live in better houses than the Russians. They dress like Americans and have churches of their own as have also the Danes, Swedes, Bohemians and Catholics.

Many farmers who had such large crops of wheat and flax last year were unable to thresh all the grain and are busy at present threshing. It is a beautiful sight to see the large fields of flax when in bloom: for miles and miles a blue velvet lawn, as it were, presents itself to our view. Here is where I analyzed my first specimen of linum or flax. Prof. Gray gives the flax as an example of a perfect or typical flower. Prof. Wood finds one objection to the above by claiming that the pistils slightly cohere at their base. He gives the crassula as the type. The idea of type was undoubtedly conceived before either the linum or crassula were created. It matters little whether found in enslaved Africa or free America, so we discover through them the Author of Nature.

The coldest weather we had was some 50° below zero. The air is, however, very dry and one scarcely believes it to be so cold until he looks at the thermometer, (which is usually graduated to 60° below zero.) Blizzards are frequent and dreaded by all. A few weeks ago we had our most severe blizzard. There was not much snow but the mercury fell so fast that one could observe it descending towards the bulb. I was about twenty miles from any town or village, on the open prairie. I had agreed to meet some of my fellow teachers in a pleasant country school house (that is, it was very pleasant for us.) For one day and a night we were shut in by the howling storm and with nothing to eat, but the second evening we decided to face the elements. Picture, if you can, a crowd of ladies and gentlemen arm in arm, with handerchiefs tied over their faces, and one (myself) with a wooden pail over his head, and you have the negative. My nose and ears were frozen before we had gone five rods. We stopped at a neighbor's who was indeed very kind to accommodate us. This was a complete "freeze out," played by teachers.

After having battled with the realities of life and visited many noted places in the Northwest the past few years, I started homeward from near Pipe Stone, in Southwestern Minnesota. Here is a ridge three miles long and twenty-five feet high, where the Indians used to congregate once a year and gather jasper for their pipes. They thought the place was sacred.

We are now going towards the Twin City by the way of Mankato, passing through the country where the James–Younger gang used to do their daring deeds. To the left a short distance is a frame house in which Frank and Jesse James stayed all night after their raid on the Northfield Bank. This is also the site of the Sioux massacre of 1862.

We are nearing Mankato, on the right bank of the Minnesota River. One of the three State Normal Schools is located here.

There are high bluffs of stone used for building purposes. A very valuable cement is also found here. Some of the varieties of timber along the Minnesota River are the red, swamp and rock elm; black, white and burr oak; spruce, fir and maple. Wild plums and mulberries are abundant. Near Kesota is an immense cream colored stone quarry. The next town is St. Peters, a beautiful place near the Minnesota River. The First Hospital for the Insane is here as is also Gustavus Adolphus College, a Lutheran institution.

A crowd of passengers are on board the train, some dressed very nicely, gentlemen with plug hats and Prince Albert coats. A young lady dressed in a long trailing silk is making herself rather conspicious; she is a special favorite with the conductor and some commercial men. At Ottawa a great pile of wood is corded to be shipped to homes on the prairies. For a few minutes I was talking to a gentleman about Fort Sisseton Reservation. He asked " Is there good land there?" "Yes sir, some excellent farming land, there are, however, many squatters there already who will have the advantage of filing claims. There will be a grand rush to this place by both male and female. It will be opened about the fifteenth of next month." At the close of our conversation there was a little excitement on the train as a man had been carried past his station and attempted to jump off, but was forced to remain until we reached Lesourd, the next station. The Superintendent of the road remarked, "I would not jump off of the train for ten dollars." Some smiled at his low estimation of life.

A deep snow drift is in this place and the section men are out clearing it from the track and depot. The train rolled on. I judge this region is rather well-to-do as their country school houses are of stone and covered with shingles. "Merriam Junction," says the conductor. The Minneapolis division goes on the west side of the river and the St. Paul road on the east. The fields are covered with large boulders left to remind the tourist that he is passing through a region where glaciers once existed. "We will soon see Fort Snelling," says my friend. I had frequently seen the picture and when I was busy recalling from memory the image, he said, "There it is." Many passengers crowded to the windows to see the real, as it is more impressive than tongue or pen can describe or portray. There are many buildings. From one the Stars and Stripes are making gentle curves in the breeze. Regiments of militia are constantly kept here to quell troubles as the one witnessed with our red brothers this winter. In 1823 the first Sunday School in Minnesota was held within the white walls of the Old Fort.

We are now nearing St. Paul. On our right are cliffs of sand stone 150 feet high, while on the left flows the Mississippi River. We pass

this beautiful scenery and the conductor calls out "Western Junction." A number of passengers alight. I look out for a moment and see that the sun is sinking. The train moves on again and now the cliffs are on the left. We pass under several long bridges which are built across our track: these seem to be thirty feet above us. On the bridges are rows of electric lights in forms of arches which look like so many stars placed in scores of rain bows. Arriving at the depot everybody is in a rush. Busses and cabs are in readiness for the passengers. St. Paul, the capital, has a population of 140,000. Nearly two hundred passenger trains leave in a day. After supper I started to visit the city, it was, however, too cold to stay out long. The people are energetic and industrious; one nice feature I noticed was that they use magic lanterns to advertise their business at night.

In order to get a view of the interior of the Grand Opera House, I concluded to go and see "The Danger Signal," a railroad play, however, not noticeably demoralizing. The building is rightly named "The Grand." It has a seating capacity of 3,000. Several hundred electric lights are formed into arches, stars and shapes of all kinds: The orchestra discoursed some very excellent music, in fact the best I had heard since leaving the University in the East. The people were dressed tastefully and almost all had opera glasses. Quite a contrast to the people in the Southwestern part of the State. I now returned to the hotel. The next morning I started for the Capitol. It is a beautiful building. The Governor's room was first visited but he had not yet arrived: leaving this place and visiting the rest of the Executive Departments, I went up stairs to the Legislative Halls. The Senate has forty-seven members and the Representatives are one hundred and three. The Historical Society, which is in the basement, was next visited. The first question I asked the Librarian was, "How many volumes are in the library?"

"Thirty-two thousand. Are you a stranger here?"

"Yes sir."

"Would you like to see our relics? There are some things you will not see in other States."

"It will afford me great pleasure to examine them."

"All right, just step to the rear of the room."

On arriving there I noticed a relic called the Old St. Paul Post-office. It had sixteen pigeon-holes and a shelf for papers, this had been used as late as 1849. Forty-three years has made quite a change. The next was the scalp and arm bones of Little Crow, the hair was as black as the feathers of a crow; a piece of the house of the first victim of the Sioux Massacre, 1862; a pre-historic water jug found in Cross County, Arkansas; a pipe smoked by Chippewa Chief, "Hole-in-the-Day;" an Indian chain made from twisted bison hair; a watch chain made of hair from Chas-ka-don, a Sioux hung at Mankato,

December 26th, 1862; an ornament made by Sitting Bull—it was intended for a cane; head of newel post from stairway in the old Provincial Government of Massachusetts built in 1634. The wood was still in good condition; bomb shells used at final storming of St. Paul " Ice Palace," January 27th, 1887; pieces of the original Atlantic Cable, laid in 1858; hand-cuffs worn by Henry Kriegler, hung at Albert Lea, March, 1861, and buried with his body nineteen years; a quill of a bald eagle; an ornamented pen holder made from the femur of a Sioux; Indian bows and arrows; a cane made from the scaffold on which thirty eight Indian murderers were hung, 1862, at Mankato, also a rope used in the execution; a small button made from the Flag Ship "Lawrence," sunk in Erie Harbor, September 10th, 1813; bones of Mound Builders, found at White Bear Lake; Dakota medicine charm, a piece of wood cut in the shape of a snake.

CABINET NO. 2.

The first relic is a revolver from the body of Clel. Miller, one of the James-Younger gang, a self cocker, center fire and 44 caliber. A linen duster worn by one of the gang at the raid on the First National Bank of Northfield, Sept. 7th, 1876. It had been worn to conceal the weapons and had been dropped in the bank as was also a sack in which they intended to put the money, but did not get any; a cubical box used for drafting men into the Union army; a British saber captured at Yorktown; a Rebel bowie knife; a grape shot of brass and copper, from the battle-field of Chapultepec, Mexico, September 13th, 1847; collection of minerals from near Leadville, Colorado; native cloth from Samoan Island; a provision basket from Fiji Islands; a small piece of flag of Morgan's Rifle Company of the Revolutionary war.

I now walked up stairs again to the Governor's room and this time he was present. An attendant introduced us and we had a very nice chat. Before leaving he presented me with his photograph and wrote on it,
Faithfully Yours,
WILLIAM MERRIAM.

From here I returned to the Senate Chamber for a short time in hopes of gathering a few notes. The Grain Inspectors were to meet but only half of them were present and they were talking politics more than business. One gentleman remarked that the State would go 12,000 Alliance. Another gentleman said the Republicans were loosing their hold. The majority thought that the Democrats would stand a good show this year. One said, "In fact all the Northwest and the South are for Cleveland."

I now leave the Capitol and take a street car for Minneapolis. To my right are two fine

THE NORTH-WEST.   17

residences, one belonging to the Governor and the other to his father. Farther on are two large brick buildings where fallen women are cared for by the Catholic Sisters. The place is called the House of Good Shepherds. Still a little farther on the same side is Hamlein University, a Methodist institution. There are three large buildings, one a massive white stone structure in which the sciences are taught. To the left is McAlister College, a Presbyterian institution. It is located on a slight elevation which gives them a beautiful campus. They have two large buildings.

We now near the Minnesota Transter, many buildings are here, one 1,500 feet long. Two hundred and fifty men are employed to transfer freight to all parts of the Union and Canada. The street car shed is the next on the left, a large white building where seventy cars are kept. This is directly between St. Paul and Minneapolis. A little farther on is an Academy. A few more minutes ride and we are in the center of the metropolis. I next boarded the cars for the far famed and beautiful resort, Minnehaha Falls. The Washburn A Mills was the next object in sight on this route. The Minnehaha Driving Park is also passed. There are not many passengers on the car and some are constantly leaving as we approach their homes. Towards the end of the five mile trip only one passenger, a gentleman, and myself were on the car. We started for the Falls together. In another moment we stood gazing on the type of the beautiful, the sparkling water makes a parabolic curve and leaps over the precipice into a cup-shaped basin sixty feet below. From here it goes between cliffs laughing and playing until it reaches the Minnesota River. The gentleman said he frequently visited the resort and in the Summer would get back of the falls to listen to the sweet music which sounded, he said, "Like sweet music of

Angels." At present the water is some lower than in the Summer. I ventured to secure a few stones from the very edge of the precipice in which I succeeded, but the gentleman told me it was a daring feat, and it took a man of nerve, "For a man some five years ago tried the same feat and lost his life." In the summer time crowds picnic in the woods where only six years ago four wigwams were still standing.

I next examined the stones of the cliffs and saw that they are sand stone of various colors. The predominating colors are those of the rain bow. This resort is frequently visited by students far and near and is the most famous falls in the world. Another view is taken of Fort Snelling, which is close to the falls, and a last glance is given the cascade as a car is entered for the Union depot. Arriving there I learn that twenty lines of railroad connect this city with the outer world.

The Mississippi lumber scene is the next attraction. The logs are floated down from the northern part of the state to be sawed by the score of mills. Millions of dollars' worth of wood floats down the river annually.

Let us next visit St. Anthony Falls. This has a water fall vastly greater than the Minnehaha. It is estimated to have a water power equal to 135,600 horse power and can run thirty mills. It descends gradually to a depth of twenty feet.

After seeing those giant mills I thought I would like to visit at least one and see the interior. So I started towards the Pillsbury, Washburn & Co.'s world renowned mill. I however visited several other places on my way as they could hardly be passed by unnoticed. The Minneapolis Exposition building, which was erected May 26th, 1886, is passed through first. It is an enormous structure, and the place is being remodeled at a cost of $10,000 to accommodate the Republican National Convention which is to convene here this year. They will undoubtedly " have plenty of room " and to spare. Nice asbestos stone walks are in front of the building.

The Century Piano Factory is visited next. They have a capital of $500,000 and manufacture the high grade Mehlin piano. A newspaper man from Oregon and myself were ushered from attic to cellar, after we had taken the elevator for the fifth floor. Here were several rooms in which were completed pianos. The gentleman played on several instruments to tone them for us. I could not see why he had brought us up here at first but it soon dawned on my mind that he was following the analytic process and noticed that had he proceeded the opposite we would have had a vague idea of the complex mechanism of a piano. The varnishing department is next visited where seven coats are applied. "How many pianos do you turn out in a week?" "We average fifteen. You see this, gentlemen," continued he, "This is a patented muffler to keep children and grown people from constantly beating on the piano without locking it."

In another department we examined many varieties of mahogany of different colors from

San Domingo. As we were passing to a lower room I asked him the price of his pianos. "The prices vary from $400 to $500." In another department a score of men are gluing the ribs on the sounding boards with bent staves propped up to the ceiling. This exerts a great pressure to the square foot on the sounding board.

The veneering process is next witnessed. Thin slices of mahogany are placed one upon the other with glue between them until the desired thickness is obtained. These boards are then dried in an oven.

Many other departments were passed through where keys, wires and other pieces were manufactured. On reaching the lower floor I asked: "How many hands do you employ?"

"We try to keep the number at 125." "Every week," continued he, "We pay them $1,500. Now let us go to the engine room." In the enginé room was a 150 horse power engine at work. We thanked the gentleman for his kindness in showing us around and my friend from Oregon went to the depot and I kept on my route.

The Union Iron Works were visited next. There are two large buildings and several departments in each building. The heavy work is done on the first floor while on the second, the light work and carpentering. One hundred and fifty men are employed. It would take an expert in this line to see the whys and wherefores, so about all I could do was to pass through and brush the flying cinders from my eyes. It was nearing the hour of six and I hastened toward the Pillsbury-Washburn mill. After receiving a pass, and registering, I stepped on the elevator and was sent to the sixth story. Here are thousands of machines run by innumerable cogs and the din was deafening. I started down a spiral stairs near the centre of the building to the fifth floor, but I did not feel quite at ease yet as the thought came to me, suppose an alarm of fire would be given, where would I be? Just then I noticed several chemical fire engines with long rubber hose attached. This gave me some courage. I noticed hundreds of Holt's purifiers at work. Each department is well illuminated with electric lights. I pass down to the fourth floor and one circle of the spiral stairs is made. At the foot was a door, I suppose to shut off the sound from above. I hardly knew whether to pass through or not, as I did not wish to enter only where I was welcome, however, I opened the door and saw that I was on the right road. I did not stay on the fourth and third floors long as the scene was only changed a little by having larger machines and my nerves were strung to the highest pitch trying to dance to the rattling of the cogs.

On the second floor is the packing department. Here are stacks of sacks and piles of barrels, many filled with the choicest flour. The first floor is the grinding room where 9,500,000 bushels of wheat are ground in a year. This is the largest mill in the world and is the eighth wonder. When I arrived at the door I observed that my Prince Albert had turned into a "miller's coat."

Returning to the hotel I ate a hearty supper, after which I read the daily papers for a short time. I then visited the museum. Here I made the acquaintance of a conductor on the Northern Pacific. We were standing near a large moose and two deers when I asked him if he had ever visited the Black Hills.

"No," says he, "but I have seen many of these animals in Wyoming and Montana."

When was you in Wyoming?

"Last Fall. I had a very narrow escape from a moose once, and I will tell it to you if you wish to hear it. I have frequently told it to newspaper men but they never get it just as it happened. If you will take it down in shorthand, I will give it just as it occurred."

All right, you have found your man this time. But this reminds me also of a moose hunt I witnessed once.

"Well, you being the older, tell your story first."

Thank you; I will then lay the tablet aside and proceed. Last Fall I started from Prairie Junction, in the south-western part of the state, to visit Salt Lake City and the National Park, in Wyoming, passing through Sioux Falls where I met a former school-mate just making a fortune in the law business. From here I went to Yankton, S. Dakota, and down to Sioux City, visiting the Corn Palace which was quite a treat.

"Then I judge you went to Omaha, Neb., for you see things there which are truly wonderful?"

Yes sir, but did not remain there long enough to visit all the places of interest. However, I visited the smelting works which are the largest in the world.

"The Union Pacific terminates here."

Yes.

"I used to work on that road also."

From here I took the train running through Northern Nebraska and noticed many nice prairie farms, with sod houses, some of which were country school houses. When I arrived at the south-western part of South Dakota my attention was attracted by the Bad Lands, which are large hills of petrified wood, wrought into all imaginable shapes. I now determined to visit the Black Hills, for I had heard and read of them for a score of years. I ascended the highest peak, called Harney's Peak, which has an elevation of about 8,000 feet. All kinds of minerals are found, including silver and gold. A great effort is being made to develop the tin mines. Some of the building materials found are marble, gypsum and sand stone. This is a splendid place to study the science of Geology. I gathered specimen rocks from the Eozoic era down to the Age of Man. I could talk for a long time about the different ages and systems, but I wish to get at the moose story. "That is just what I am patiently waiting for." I am almost to the place, so leaving the Black Hills I passed over to Wyoming through the place where Custer had his last engagement with the Indians, and on towards the Big Horn Mountains where my hunt is located.

I went out one day with a number of scouts and railroad men to enjoy a hunt. " Well you enjoyed it I suppose" remarked my friend, laughing. Yes sir, better than one of our company. One of the rules was that each person should have three shots. The one being closes to the game should have the first chance. There was a young man—in fact you resemble him some—well I believe you are the gentleman; I thought I recognized the face. "Well, proceed. It is nice to hear some one else relate our own misfortunes. You will not need the short hand in this case as the facts are indelibly fixed in your memory." All right I will proceed and make it short. You watch whether I tell it correctly. We were to have three shots—you fired at a passing deer and killed it. Yes, we had fresh venison for dinner. Then all at once the hound began to bark as if certain death was near, you became somewhat excited and fired your second shot just as a loud "Mu" sounded over the hill. Instead of aiming at the oncoming moose you shot the dog. In another instant the moose was rushing towards you and you fired your third shot which pierced its shoulder blade. This only enraged the beast and you swung yourself out of danger by catching an overhanging limb when I fired my first shot which, however, did not seem to pacify his mind. So the animal backed a few steps from the tree and ran forward with such a speed and striking the tree such a blow as

to cause you to loose your hold and you fell directly in front of the enraged moose which was attempting to gore you, when a second ball from my rifle pierced its heart.

" Yes, that was a close call for me. You remember we started back together on the branch to Cheyenne and I had to make my run the next day towards the coast." Yes, and I started to Denver, Colorado, and down to Colorado Springs; then taking the road through Leadville, passing the Mountains of the Holy Cross, finally entering Utah, and remaining a few days in Salt Lake City.

One of the principal features here are the Mormons. "Did you visit the Salt Lake?" Yes sir! I learned the lake had an area of 3.000 square miles and the water varied in depth from 12 to 70 feet. There are also shrimps and different kinds of insects to be found in the water. I thought I would take a bath in the saline water for I had frequently heard that a person could not drown in salt water. But I found that unless a person knew enough about the invigorating exercise, he would not float like an egg—but his head would be in the water and his feet in the air, which would not be a very agreeable attitude for any length of time. I also noticed a perceptible dryness of the atmosphere which explains the rapid evaporation which is observed in this region.

The capital has a present population of 45,000. Here, I was told, lived a Methodist minister who was a school-mate of mine. If I do not stop soon, we will not see much of the museum tonight. "Go on and tell about the rest of the trip; where did you go from Salt Lake City?" I went north through Idaho, then to Butte City, Montana, and visited the great smelting establishments, found here. Such billows of smoke issue from the numerous smelters that it is disagreeable at times to live here.

Next I went southwards towards the Park. It has an area of 3,600 square miles and reaches an elevation of 12,000 feet. The place has been set apart by Congress as a National resort. The Yellowstone Lake was visited which has an elevation of one and one-half miles above the sea level.

The falls and Grand Canon were also visited. I next went to the head waters of the Madison River, which rises in the Park, and viewed some of the noted geysers, arriving just in time to see the Giant, the most remarkable as well as the most popular, send up boiling streams to the height of 140 feet. The best comparison I can make is, it looked like a gas well when it is "shot," and the mud and water is forced upwards by the dynamite.

I met several Indians in this part of the state, but none offered to take my scalp. A few bison and many antelopes are seen in this vicinity.

I now take the Northern Pacific and pass through the Crow Reservation in Montana. Farther on, near the boundary of Montana and North Dakota, is the Mandan Indian Reservation.

"What is your conclusion concerning the present Indians?"

To say the least, they are not savage nor fierce if the whites deal with them fairly.

I saw some out farming and trying to earn their own living. I visited a camp and must acknowledge that many were more civilized than the whites.

The squaws and children were keeping the birds away from the ripened grain, a few were reading, while some of the young men were amusing themselves horse back riding and shooting mark.

Every young lady, when she arrives at a certain age, has a pet dog, so in this respect she is up to the standard of civilization (?)

A short time was spent in Bismarck and I then started for the south-western part of Minnesota, to engage in teaching. "Let us look around here a few moments and see what they have," said my friend.

All right, here is a lady snake charmer. The next attraction were cages of monkeys, squirrels and birds. The former for some reason can always hold an audience. The next was a middle aged lady with whiskers long enough for the breeze to play with them. The next was a scout with long hair reaching down to his back. It was very interesting to hear him talk about his adventures. We now leave the museum and are on the street again.

After a dozen unsuccessful attempts to find a church where we might go and listen to something elevating, we gave up in despair and followed the crowd. We soon learned that they were not the class who attend churches but typical theatre goers. On arriving at the Hall, I managed to get a glimpse of the interior and took in the situation at a glance. On the stage were eleven rather respectably dressed women, surrounded by the stars and stripes. While the audience, men and women alike, were drinking and smoking cigars and cigarettes.

My friend and I concluded that this was not the place for enlightened American citizens, and to not insult the flag with our presence, so we started for the hotel.

In the morning I took an early train back to St. Paul. Before starting I thought I would purchase a tablet so that I might take notes on the way, as my old one was completely filled. I entered every drug and stationery store for blocks but could not find a tablet. In fact one dealer had the courage to ask what they were. I was finally directed to a book-bindery.

On arriving at the place I saw one small tablet lying on the shelf and asked the proprietor whether he kept tablets for sale. He looked at me as though he had a curious customer for once, and said "Yes sir; do you wish to buy some?" Well, are you doing a wholesale or retail business? For my part I would be contented to get one or a piece of paper. "Here is one; will this suit you? It has been used some but there are still many leaves in the back part." All right, what is it worth?

"I guess you can take it along for ten cents." I thanked him for his two cent tablet and remarked that had I a few more moments time I would go over to Minneapolis and purchase a dozen and present them to the dealers as relics.

After purchasing a ticket to Madison, Wis. for $7.80 and getting my trunk and valise checked, all is in readiness and soon I am going again.

The first city of interest is Northfield, which has a population of 3,300. It is beautifully located in the valley of the Cannon river. Carleton college has a large observatory and furnishes standard time to the North-west.

As we approach Faribault the surface becomes more uneven, but the city itself is located on a delta on the east side of the Straight river.

Its population is 6,500. The several asylums for the Blind, Deaf and Imbecile are located here. The Seabury Divinity School, also a St· Mary's Hall are located in the city.

The fruit boy is coming with apples. They are almost a curiosity to me; an ordinary sized apple costs 5 cents. A large crowd of passengers are on the train. As we near Owatonna some students alight to attend the Academy. The town is about the size of Northfield. Many visitors are attracted by the medical springs. Farther on I noticed a barn yard filled with

cattle, sheep and swine, the braver ones venturing out to nip the first blades of grass in the bright sunlight of the coming Spring.

We are now at Ramsey. The conductor

THE NORTH-WEST.   33

says "Take car ahead; 20 minutes for dinner." I recall to memory that I passed through this region last Summer from Milwaukee to La Crosse westward. I arrived in the latter city as the sun was setting. The first place I visited was the "Father of Waters." I took a seat on the left bank of the river and was filled with joy at the beautiful scene as I looked across the water westward. The sinking sun still sparkling in the slowly flowing water and across on the right bank were the beautiful green prairies and forests of Minnesota while around me were tall, massive buildings reflecting the last rays of sunlight from Wisconsin soil, back to the boats afloat on the bosom of the great river. After supper I visited the city which has a population of 25,000. At about midnight the train left for the West passing almost the whole distance a little north of Iowa. One of the passengers was a lady who was going to Spring Valley. She claimed to be a Christian Scientist. When the train arrived at Winnebago the day was dawning and from there on towards Pipe Stone many nice prairie homes were passed. Along the Des Moines river is grand scenery.

Jackson, the county seat of Jackson county, is located in a valley with a ridge surrounding it, so that a person can scarcely see the town from the train. As I neared Prairie Junction I concluded that the place was rightly named "Prairie Junction," for several prairies seemed to be joined together. The lake we see from the Junction is Heron Lake where the sportsmen can enjoy shooting wild geese which are so numerous on the water that they give it the appearance of a large feather bed. Ducks, gulls and prairie chickens are also very numerous; in fact they obscure the sun and protect the farmers from becoming sun struck. Fishes of all kinds can be caught here without bait. The fishermen merely walk to the edge of the water where they are patiently waiting to be picked up. Many wolves and badgers are found but they are not very savage. Some call this "the land of the plentiful" but it is better known to me as the "Blue grass Valley;" that is, a person gets the "blues" for coming to the "grass valley." After arriving at the Junction I continued on my route westward, through Sioux Falls, but passed through this region again in a week on my way to the college.

As I was waiting for a train to take me to the college, in which I was employed as instructor in the sciences, I beheld a small dark cloud, as it were, in the distance; the blackness came nearer and nearer and to my surprise discovered that what I supposed to be a cloud proved to be millions of crows. They kept up their flight westward for two hours and were so thick that their wings over-lapped like shingles on a roof.

I soon arrived at my place of duty. The College, if we may so call it, is located in a little country town in the "Blue grass Valley." On alighting at the station I noticed that the post-office was in the same room with the telegraph office, and going in inquired for the allwise principal. I was told by the post master that he was here cancelling stamps. After a short time we started in a farm wagon to the college buildings.

I noticed two buildings, one a small dormatory for the boys and the other was used for various purposes. In the basement was the kitchen, on the first floor a few school rooms and bed room for some of the teachers, also a music hall 8 by 10 feet. On the second floor is the ladies' department, while on the third floor a few store boxes are arragned and labeled "College bank," "Post office." I was finally assigned a room in the dormatory so that I could watch the boys and keep them under subjection. The school was run on the Charles Dickens plan, more of the latter than Charles.

While here I held the following honorable positions, in their order: First instructor, then janitor, librarian, hostler and farmer.

I remember one day I made the statement that in agricultural colleges wheat was being planted like corn and the experiment proves that a larger yield is produced, and the grains larger and more plump. The would-be professors only hooted at the idea and remarked, "no one is foolish enough to believe this." I was surprised that they were a half century behind the times but soon noticed the cause for this, for when I visited the library to read up some late articles, which I was in hopes of finding, I only found a few old magazines which had been preserved as relics, from their school days. The meals consisted of decayed fish, "treacle," and butter so strong that it had the power to change from a yellow to a light blue color.

There were some fifty shoats running around the yard which would enter the kitchen where the potatoes and vegetables were kept. After the pigs had selected the best, the rest were prepared for the students. The farmer president believes in putting the theory into practice immediately: e. g. if the word "jack rabbit" comes up in the class, he immediately sends them out on a jack rabbit hunt, so when a dozen are caught he will have an excuse to go to town, a distance of ten miles, which usually takes up the rest of the day.

The twenty minutes are up and the train is moving towards Austin. Several railroads center here. It has a population of 2,500 and is located on the Red Cedar river which affords excellent water power. Two students, a lady and gentleman, who are sitting two seats back of me are talking about some literary and criticizing their superiors. The lady uses the phrase, "that is fun," very frequently. " The boys could not *ketch* him." says the gentleman.

We now pass by a nice farm house with evergreens on both sides of the road leading to the house. Many wind and snow breaks are along the track. A big black dog is running out from a farm house to bark at the passing train. We now pass a white, frame Norwegian church. A small town is passed where nothing of importance could be seen only a dozen men and boys standing at the depot passing away their precious moments by cutting tobacco chips. A lady to my right is reading a novel. Two seats in front of me is a rather good looking young lady, dark curly hair, and wearing a white face veil. At Leroy the gentleman student alights. He gives a final pleasant look, tips his hat and all is over.

We are now crossing the Minnesota and Iowa line. Lime Spring is a beautiful small village. Several loaded wagons with flour are standing at the station. There is also a nice race track near the edge of the town. On the bluff, to the left, is a cemetery. Instead of having a "blue and gray" appearance it looks "green and white." Cresco is a nice town with many beautiful structures. The lady student alighted here. The ground in this vicinity is level.

The train is running so swiftly that shorthand can not be used, in fact my long hand writing is unusually long. Conover is a railroad junction. The lady who was reading the novel got off here. Almost all the passengers who got on at St. Paul have alighted but myself and the lady with the white veil. She has now changed one seat nearer to me. A fire along the track is sending up a cheering blaze as we pass by, while on the opposite side of the track lie high snow drifts.

At Calmar several exchanged cars for Fayette to attend school. A gentleman tells me that we are now in Clay county, Iowa. After pass-

ing a few more small stations we near one of the most beautiful regions of the North-west. Every one is waking up to see the natural scenery. The lady in front and myself have started up a conversation. A gentleman sitting back of me tapped me on the shoulder and said "Do you see those cliffs yonder? In a few moments we will pass through there. Here is where Black Hawk was caught." Another elderly gentleman said "This is where Jeff. Davis made his elopement with his future wife."

Well, says I, we can't blame them, for it is certainly a very romantic place. If I had half a chance I would try it myself; at this we all had a hearty laugh and we felt more at ease. Even the lady, who was very modest and reserved, smiled an approval. The elderly gentleman said "The train used to run so slow when the soldiers returned from the war that they would stop to saw wood and let the car get ahead then catch it again."

We now pass through bluffs of lime stone 300 ft. high. "McGregor," calls out the conductor. As soon as the train stopped I ran to the closest bluff and broke off a small fragment to keep as a relic. I fired one shot at the overhanging bluff merely imagining an Indian hiding behind the rocks. After passing a triangular building, used as a depot, we started to cross the Mississippi river, which is about

18 feet deep at this point and one-half mile wide. There is an old pontoon bridge to the left of the one on which we were. I fired a second shot in the river below in memory of De Soto, although the honor of discovering this mighty river is given by some to Alonzo de Pineda, a Spaniard, who, in 1519, sailed up its mouth and visited some of the villages along its shores and traded with the natives. A steam boat, the City of McGregor, was resting on the bosom of this renowned river.

A few rods to the left of the old bridge lies a beautiful small island; at her landing stood an ice bound steamer. Arriving at Prairie du Chien I took supper at the Sherman House and had the best meal I ever had in the West for 25 cents.

At the table sat an old gentleman who had lived in the city ever since the time the mail had been carried by post to St. Paul. He could tell interesting things about the Black Hawk war, Jeff. Davis, Pres. Tyler, for he had known all of them. He said Jeff. Davis and Tyler were at the Fort with the soldiers, Davis being an officer under Tyler. The young officer fell in love with Tyler's daughter, but his attentions paid to the lady were not approved of by Mr. Tyler. So the young soldier concluded to set a night and elope with his lady. She had been kept in the house on the second story for a long time, but Davis was not to be outgeneraled in this style, so he employed two Indians to bring two boats and wait until he should return. In the meantime Davis went to Tyler's residence and assisted her to descend by means of ropes. They were then rowed to a minister's and married. This event disturbed the confidence of Tyler in Davis and for a long time he was not recognized by Tyler as his son-in-law.

Some time after this event Davis was fighting the Indians and won, not only a laurel for himself, but for the nation. He received the praise of his father-in-law, who concluded that Davis was a better judge of human nature than himself. After this they became firm friends.

Black Hawk was captured near Broad-ax as he was trying to cross the Mississippi river.

After supper, as the shades of darkness were gathering around, like a dark pall, enshrouding the historic monument of nature and the unnumbered tombs of friend and foe, I cast a last glance across the "Father of Waters," McGregor and the "Hawkeye State."

Prairie du Chien has a population of 4,000. The town is older than Philadelphia but has no manufactories and consequently the rising generations go to other cities for employment. A Catholic college is located here.

I now take the train for Madison, Wisconsin.

Not much of interest is seen on this route as it is night and the moon did not make her appearance until a late hour. We passed through Wanzeka, a small village, about 8 P. M. We next passed through Spring Green, a beautiful little town which makes a nice picture as the rising moon is coming over the ridge and welcomed by the baying of the village dogs. The news agent, who seemed a good young man, sat down by my side and we passed the next hour in relating our hardships and finally ended up with our travels. "We learn a great deal by traveling," says he, "Not so much book knowledge but when a person has traveled extensively and met all classes of people, he generally can make a living for himself." Yes, in my judgment there is a great deal of benefit derived in traveling, especially if one observes closely. Would you like to hear of my recent trip to the North-west?

"Yes sir, I would be pleased to hear it."

Well, a few weeks ago I started from near Fort Sisseton Reservation, up to Winnipeg, Manitoba, Canada. Do you know what Manitoba means? "No sir." Well, it is an old Indian name and the Sioux, or Dakotas, called it Minne-topa, meaning the four waters or lakes Winnipegosis, Winnipeg, St. Martin, Manitoba. Here I noticed many foreigners, especially Russians. The soil produces the best crops of wheat in the world. Winnipeg, the capital, has a population of 22,000. It is sometimes called the "Gate City of the North-west." I now started to the coast on the Canada Pacific.

There are many nice prairie homes in Assiniboia and Alberta. The Indians are in the majority over the whites, of which the Black Feet tribes are the more numerous. In this region are still seen forts where a fur trade is carried on with the Hudson Bay Company. The Indians and Creoles exchange the skins of beavers, minks and foxes for the necessaries and luxuries of life.

Entering British Columbia one beholds beautiful scenery. In passing the Selkirk Mountains " the loop," is the principal attraction. Large quantities of gold, silver and lead are found in the Frazer Valley. There are still unexplored regions near the waters of this river and on northward.

Arriving at Vancouver Island I took a ship, passing by Victoria, the capital of British Columbia, through Juan de Fuca strait, out on the Pacific Ocean, headed for Sitka, Alaska. This was a pleasant trip as the climate was not so severe as I had anticipated for the temperature is modified by the warm current from Japan.

Good accommodations were had at rather exorbitant rates. Most of the time we were sailing close to the Canadian shore and nothing of unusual interest was observed until we were nearing Prince of Wales Island where a few grizzly bears were noticed on the coast. Just before we arrived at Sitka an interesting spectacle presented itself to our view. There were two small boats a short distance from us and we could hear the men shouting to each other through their trumpets. In an instant there arose out of the water a huge mass of something about the size of a barn. At this same moment a volley of shots were fired from the two boats, and it dawned on my mind that the monster was a whale and had been killed by the whalers. It was supposed that he had strayed away from his companions in the Arctic Ocean and passed through the Behring strait, and came down to "The Peaceful" intending to raise a disturbance.

When the boats arrived at Sitka, I examined some of their guns. Each charge consisted of one pound of powder, an instead of using a bullet they used a spear shaped bomb with a fuse which is lighted by the burning powder. Several of these bombs are shot into the whale, the bombs exploding and killing the creature. The skin and whale bone is nearly one foot in thickness. I was very anxious to examine his teeth and see what chances a person had to pass through a live whale's mouth, unharmed.

I noticed the whale had fifty-two large ivory teeth, the largest teeth being six inches long and weighing three pounds each. While here I also examined a small can of ambergris from a sperm whale. The can would probably hold eight ounces and was valued at eighty dollars per ounce. The whalers keep actual account of all whales killed, where, when, the size, etc., the same as book keepers do in mercantile business.

Sitka, the capital, has a population of 1,000. Outside of the tropics this is the rainiest place in the world. It has an annual precipitation reaching ninety inches, and rain three days out of four.

The Governor has his headquarters here and receives a salary of $3,000. The seat of the Bishop of the Greek Church is also here. The inhabitants are whites, Indians and Creoles. The principal occupation is fishing and hunting, although farming is carried on in some localities, the principal cereals raised being barley and oats.

The Indians of Alaska are divided into families, each family has a badge or totem pole of carved wood, some reaching the height of 60 feet. These poles are ornamental. Some of the figures carved on them are the forms of eagles, wolves and bears. These are also used instead of monuments.

The next day I visited the Thousand Islands. This is a group of small islands resembling an archipelago. The sleds, I noticed, were not like ours; they had no iron runners but slats instead, which were tied on by means of rawhide. The inhabitants principally live on seals and sea birds. The Esquimaux can eat ten pounds of whale or an equal amount of reindeer at one meal. I was told that the children seldom have candy or sweet meats on Christmas but are presented with an extra pint of blubber on this occasion. Instead of gas and electric lights they place some moss in a basin of blubber which serves as a light. "They say there is a vast resource of timber in Alaska."

Yes sir, that is true; in places however there are timberless regions but around Sitka grows the spruce and yellow cedar in vast forests. Some of the spruce grows to the enormous height of 240 feet. The yellow cedar is the most valuable on account of taking a ready polish and thus becoming valuable as a cabinet wood. The fir and hemlock is also found in large quantities. There is not much danger of the forests being destroyed by fire like in regions more southerly, as the air is moist and the ground is covered with moss.

In the warmer season, in many parts of Alaska, are seen large lakes filled with floating timber. Here, in Summer blooms the wild rose and the robin sings to the natives while the mosquito sends in his bill. Squirrels are scarce but moose are plentiful. A story is afloat, told by Lieutant Schwatka, that on his expeditions he saw natives shoot a squirrel with a 10-guage Winchester shot gun, the cartridge weighing more than the carcass.

"What about the Behring Sea question?" This is the most important question in the North-west at the present time. There are many views taken by the inhabitants, some belligerent while others of calmer minds desire arbitration and let the pen settle the difficulty, instead of the sword. It is a regretted fact by the better class of people, both Canadian and Americans, that many of the hundreds of sealing vessels attack seal herds in the Behring Sea each year, when the fur seal is migrating and frequently many of the females are destroyed in mere sport while she is out hunting food for herself and young ones, thus injuring the fur seal industry. Just what will be the outcome of this difficulty is at present a matter of conjecture but nothing serious is likely to result.

President Harrison and Lord Salisbury, the Prime Minister, although both great men and wise in many things, made mistakes which are not commendable to diplomats. President Harrison claimed the whole Northern Pacific

Ocean and tried to wall it in with a peculiar kind of a fence so as to let the seals from Asia and British Columbia come through and also keep those from Alaska's shores at home. It was on this line of thought that Mr. Blaine showed his superiority of statesmanship over the former. Because some of their domiciles were on our shores was not sufficient proof to justify us to claim all the fur seals found in the Northern Pacific, nor to devolve us in a war with England.

One mistake of Lord Salisbury was that the Canadians might continue killing the seals while the United States and Canada or England were discussing propositions to save the seals from becoming exterminated.

I now boarded a steamer and sailed to Astoria, Oregon. On my way back I noticed a few sea lions and the rest of the voyage was sky and water. Astoria has a population of 2,800. In 1811 John Jacob Astor established a fur trading port here. I next visited Walla Walla, in the state of Washington, where I saw beautiful farms. Indeed it is an oasis between mountains; the land, however, is very high in price.

Here I took the train to Salem, where I stopped a short time. The city has a population of 5,000. It became the seat of government in 1860. The flowers were in bloom and the birds were singing to their mates. I next secured a ticket to Sacramento and paid dear for it, too, for there is only one road, and they have a monopoly. The most interesting things I observed in California were the monarch trees, known as sequoya gigantea. They are near the Sierra Nevada Mountains. I noticed one tree which was still standing and the lower part was being used for a house. A little farther on a road was made through a standing tree; I judge the tree was 300 feet high.

The train stopped a few minutes and the opportunity was improved by examining a lately fallen tree from which a large log had been cut for some purpose. I counted the wood circles of the trunk and perceived the number to be 1,896. It began its marvelous growth therefore the same year Christ was born. I stepped off the length of the tree and ascertained its length to be 400 feet—one foot of growth for each year since the discovery of America by Columbus.

Sacramento was next visited. It has a population of 26,000 and is situated on the Sacramento River, about 125 miles from the Pacific Ocean. A little east of the capital are petrified forests. There are also fossil remains of marine animals in this vicinity. A number of Chinese are living here but the bulk of them are found in San Francisco.

From here I took the Central Pacific through Nevada, passing by Lake Tahoe, up to Salt Lake City.

From this place a train was taken for Colorado. Creed, the great booming camp, was next visited. I did not remain long but saw Bob Ford, the murderer of Jesse James, who was here, it is claimed carrying on a profitable gambling business. The town has grown to 6,000 inhabitants within three months. Malaria is raging caused by the dampness of the houses which were erected out of newly sawn logs. There are also many immoral women here; in fact a virtuous woman would not enter such a hoodlum of a place for all the gold found. From here I went to the southwestern part of Minnesota and on my way to the Twin City.

"That was quite a trip and very interesting."

Yes, and I have omitted several things which I would have mentioned had I more time, but we must be almost to Madison?

"Yes sir, the next town is Black Earth, and in a few more minutes we will be at the Capital."

Arriving at Madison I went directly to a hotel and retired for the night. The next morning, after breakfast, I started for the capitol. This is a fine, large building, with marble floor. After looking around on the first floor for a short time I went to the second where the science and art gallery, senate and assembly halls are located. I first visited the Senate Chamber which faces towards the east. As I entered the door I beheld in front the motto, " Forward, 1858." Around the wall was a row of writing desks and nice settees used by the 33 members. There were also about 200 chairs in the Chamber. Two large artificial gas chandeliers were swinging from the center of the ceiling. When I was being ushered to the Assembly Hall I was informed that the present Governor, Geo. W. Peck, received a salary of $5,000 and his Lieutenant was Mr. Johnes. Arriving at the Assembly Hall I noticed the place was similar to the Senate Chamber only the things were not as tastefully arranged. One hundred members belong to this department.

I next go down stairs and visit the library which has a collection of 175,000 volumes of books and 25,000 volumes of periodicals bound in book form.

Let us now take the elevator, which is run by water power, and go to the second floor once more to visit the science and art gallery, as the doors are now opened. Taking my position at the entrance I observed the gallery had three rooms. I took the center one first. On the left side, on the wall were two rows of portraits of noted men, thirteen in each row. I did not have time to measure the proportions of the paintings, (as did our distinguished inventor at the Paris Exposition, then decided many of the master pieces to be failures,) although many of them were undoubtedly unproportionate, they yet spoke volumes to me by their expressions. The first one was that of Mar. M. Jackson; directly above him was Moses M. Strong. Continuing viewing the rest until I arrived at the rear where the portraits of S. S. Merril and Alex Mitchell were viewed. On a roller was the picture of Thomas Hood. There were also a group of smaller pictures in one frame, one a Zoandvoost fish-woman with a basket on her back. Below were pictures of guards. Another picture of interest was that of Horatius Gates on his steed. Nathaniel Green, Maj. Gen. U. S. Army, standing by the side of his horse with sword in his left hand and a three cornered hat in his right.

There were some splendid pictures of Patrick Henry and Horace Greeley. The next was a relic of the Scotch Rebellion, a portion of an old red silk flag, date in gilt figures 1719, with Latin motto, "*Neum; me impune lacessit.*" Translated, no one provokes me with impunity. The order of the Thistle was instituted by Achaius, the King of Scots, in memory of the appearance of a bright crown in the heavens. Photographs from the different Senators from 1868 also of 1883 were shown. The south side has now been viewed with the exception of one more roller. A piece of the first yard of cotton cloth woven in Wisconsin, May 26th, 1875, at Janesville. President Jefferson's inaugural speech on a piece of newspaper of two columns, each column about five inches wide and the names of the printers in the center of the column, they were, however, too dim to be read. Old Abe, is the title of a picture of an eagle, sitting on a cannon under the blue sky. This eagle was captured in the Spring of 1861, in Chippewa county, Wisconsin by an Indian named A-ge-mah-me-ge-zhig, (no wonder he could catch the young eagle.) The Indian sold it for a bushel of corn to Mr. McCann. It was concluded that the eagle should go to war, so it was bought by Company C, 8th Wis. Reg. He was sworn in by putting around his neck red, white and blue ribbons. He went through the war and it was frequently the source of great joy to the tired soldiers to have a living eagle to cheer them on. The company received an offer of $500. for him but would not part with him under any circumstances. It is said by one that his feathers are scattered all over the Union. A deed of land in Medford, Massachusetts, dated in 1662, on unruled and uncalendered paper, and not a printed letter in the heading, body or seal. The letters were not strictly English nor German but more of a mixture. The small "*r*" in Medford and other words, was the same as the present script *r* in the German. A photograph of the first settlers of Milwaukee. Photograph of the house in which the first Territorial Legislature was held at Belmont, Lafayette Co., Wis., 1836, a two story, rickety frame house. Portrait of Col. Tarleton also of Gov. Dewitt Clinton, of the State of New York. Photograph of his excellency, John Adams, President of the U. S. An India ink panel portrait of Mrs. C. A. P. Chester, one-fifth life size, arrayed in the costume she wore while engaged in her mission of love in the army hospital.

Let us now turn towards the front. On our left we see two more rows of portraits, fourteen in each row, making twenty-eight more oil paintings to be viewed, some of them being Mr. Spooner; Benj. Hopkins; Simeon Mills, a pioneer of Madison in 1837. At the front are nearly a score of portraits promiscuously arranged, also a few costly busts. In the center of the room are relics. Fossils in blue shale from Kansas City, Mo.; a ten armed creature imprinted on a flat stone; specimens of univalves, a piece of pottery from the ancient Roman city of Silchester, in Berkshire, England; bricks and flints from the walls of the ancient city Verulamium, now St. Albans, in Hertfordshire, Eng.; Ireland—a black thorn shillalah, from the Killarney Fair, 1891; a figure of Christ carved in wood, from the sixteenth century crucifix. The nails were still in his hands and feet although one of the arms was broken off. The wood at this place was worm

eaten. The features were strikingly expressive and must have been the master work of an Xylographer; a piece of the Blarney stone, it is said that he who kisses it becomes eloquent.

Kentucky is represented by a lock of hair from Daniel Boone, (they were light colored) also pieces of the hearthstone from his cabin. A cast of his skull which shows the developments of a hunter from a phrenological view; a small, egg shaped stone supposed to be a "what-is-it." Petrified wood with two cuts made by a stone ax, from Yellowstone Park. The question arose in my mind who swung the ax, when and why? A stone ax or wedge, 3 inches by $9\frac{1}{4}$ inches long found on the surface of the ground in Barrow Co., Wis., a quarter of a century ago; a large collection of coins, almost all nations and tribes being represented. A case of thirteen Roman coins, very ancient and corroded; two coins from Liberia, dated 1862; several coins from France, Switzerland, the Island of Man, also some from St. Helena, where Napoleon and the Missionary, Mrs. Judson, are buried. One conquered with the sword the other with the spirit. A Roman coin of the Reign of Tragan, found near the great Pyramids; one quarter Anna, 1862; a Spanish crown piece dated, 1776; wampum, shells and beads; American coins before 1800; a large collection of medals, badges; U. S. paper money from three cents, upwards; pre-historic copper beads, worn by some beautiful female Mound Builder, while her fingers were weaving articles of apparel on the shuttles or grinding golden

THE NORTH-WEST.

maize with a pestle while her husband was busy making axes and spades of stone or knives and spears of copper; a barbed spear, 10 inches long, found in Merton, Waukesha county in 1877; a copper spear $12\frac{1}{4}$ inches long; an adzshaped relic made of copper, weighing $4\frac{3}{4}$ lbs., the blade at the edge 5 in., at the opposite end 2 in., found south of Neileville. There was no place, however, for a handle, as we have in later days. It is supposed to have been used by a carpenter Mound Builder.

The next are old newspapers and books. The first is the New England Courant, 1722; the sermons of Albertus Magnus, published in Cologne, 1474; Pennsylvania Gazette, published by Benj. Franklin, 1739–40; I copied the following from one of the pages

"On Saturday next will be published Poor Richard's Almanack, for the year 1740. Printed and sold by the printer himself." The Book of Hours, on vellum or calf skin, written with

a quill 1386, in Latin and French; a Dutch Bible, published in 1748, profusely illustrated with full copper-plate engravings; the Nuremburg Chronicle, in Latin, printed 1493 containing 2,250 pictures, some of them painted by Nohlgemuth, the Master of Albert Durer. The picture I admired particularly was the *Ultima Aetas Mundi*, translated,—The Last Age of the World. This book is a great rarity. Specimens of writings from noted men, the women, if you will excuse the expression, are not yet "supposed to be in it:" Washington Irving, Geo. Bancroft, Oliver Holmes, John Q. Adams, Horace Greeley, U. S. Grant, a letter from Gen. Lafayette when in Paris, April 10th, 1832; a letter written by Jeff Davis in the decline of life. Also a letter from Abraham Lincoln, written in the Civil War; Alexander Hamilton, Oct. 7th, 1795; Aaron Burr. The last was from George Washington, which was according to the scripture, "The first shall be last and the last first." The phrase below is copied from his letter "this 16th of December, 1764." His "f" in the word "of" resembled a distorted figure 8 with a cipher before it. Mr. Greeley's writings were certainly not written with the intention to be read by this generation, but to be laid away and in future years be brought forth and deciphered as hieroglyphics of the Dark Age of Penmanship. In another case are beads from Sandwich Islands, two kinds, one resembling small white shells, the others look like small red beans. Japanese cloth, made by natives; the cloth was made from the bark of a tree and worn by both sexes, answering for apparel. Specimens of Maro, to cover the loins, used by natives of Tahiti, some of yellow and blue, others of red and white; a Turkey set of revenue stamps, different colored pieces of paper with certain black marks on each; a war club used by the natives of South Pacific Islands, nicely carved and ornamented; Chinese shoes, one of which, formerly worn by a Chinese belle, was about 5 inches long and would be too small for an American girl nine years old. The body of the shoe was of rich blue cloth and nicely adorned with gold ornaments. The more common shoes have wooden soles one-half inch thick; cuneiform inscriptions from the walls of the ancient city, Ninevah; newspapers from Morocco, Africa and China, Asia.

Let us now visit the room west of the center. Here is a large wooden anchor which looks as though it might have been used by Noah to anchor the Ark on Mt. Ararat. A little to the right of this, near the corner, stands a red wheel barrow to remind the visitor of the Cleveland-Blaine campaign; Mr. Roach bet on Blaine and had to wheel the barrow from a neighboring town, to Madison, while his friend, Mr. Hutchison, accompanied him and kept the barrow oiled. This created quite a sensation when they entered the city Dec. 6th, 1884. In the corner stood a Confederate torpedo constructed from a beer keg. Some of the oil paintings adorning this department are those of Keokuk, chief of the Sacs and Foxes; Pocahontas, the daughter of Powhatan, who was an Algonquin chief, she who, when appearing in London in the beginning of the sixteenth century, was called "Lady Rebecca," takes her position near that of the famous leader, Black Hawk. The next is a large painting of the Battle Ax battle ground. Near here were cases in which relics of wars are kept. A gun barrel used in Queen Anna's war, 1702–13. The gun had perhaps been used February, 1704, by one of the 350 French and Indians in the pine forests of Deerfield, Mass., and who killed 47 New Englanders and captured 112. A long octagonal gun barrel used on the Battle Ax battle ground in which Black Hawk took a prominent part in 1832. A breast-plate from the body of Col. Rogers, of the Confederate army, killed at the second battle of Corinth, Oct. 4th, 1862; broken near the center, near which were also two other deep dints caused by bullets. A military coat and chapeau of Gov. Henry Dodge, worn when fighting the wild tribes at the head waters of the Arkansas and Platte Rivers, in 1834-35. Slave whips, some with platted lashes, others with a strap similar to a razor strop, fastened to a handle. One can hardly imagine the pain these poor negroes were in after receiving forty lashes from the hand of a task master which were found in the North as well as in the South. Sword of Capt. Thos. Harvey, used in the Revolutionary war. Sword

used by Capt. John Brown, also in the Revolutionary war. These relics remind one of Paul Revere's ride, Washington and his soldiers at Valley Forge and the final separation of the colonies from the mother country. A sword used in the war of Napoleon I. by Jacob Pistorius. Sections of saplings cut off by bullets, July 22d, 1864, near Atlanta. Near these saplings McPherson was killed. Bateau used by the French fur traders on the Wisconsin waters and the Great Lakes. It was 30 feet long and could convey 18 men, two in a seat, besides a stock of goods to carry on a barter with the Indians. Wisconsin under French dominion, as shown by a silver cross. Another cross made out of wood and used by J. Baptiste L'ecuyer, a French creole, at Portage, Wis. A

chip from the U. S. Frigate Constitution, better known as "Old Ironside." On August 19th, 1812, Capt. Isaac Hull, nephew of the cowardly Gen. Hull, made himself renowned by the naval victory between his ship, the American frigate Constitution, and the English ship Guerriere. A silver coat button worn by Daniel Boone with the monogram " D. B." Two sleigh bells presented by the wife of Alexander Hamilton, to her son, Milton S. Hamilton. Two powder horns of Daniel Boone, nicely ornamented with figures and buildings cut on the horns; they first belonged to his elder brother Is. Boone, and therefore bear the monogram "I. B." A piece of the famous charter oak. Here, Capt. Wadsworth's name became immortal by his seizing the document and carrying it away to the hollow oak, afterwards known as the Charter Oak. A piece of wood from Inde-

pendence Hall, perhaps from the belfry where one hundred and sixteen years ago, the bell rang out her cheerful tidings of "Proclaim liberty throughout all the land unto all the inhabitants thereof." A piece of wood from the grave of Roger Williams, the eloquent minister who advanced the theory that each person should think for himself on subjects regarding religious matters, and he alone be responsible to his conscience. He soon fled and found refuge with the Indians, Canonicus aiding him in forming a settlement which was appropriately called Providence.

A Confederate flag captured at Tulelo, Mississippi, July 14th, 1864. Another one with the motto, "Give us a chance in the picture near the flashing of the guns." This was so riddled with bullets that it was almost impossible to read it. Confederate paper money from $1.00 upwards. A large piece of Jeff. Davis' mantle piece from his residence, 30 miles below Vicksburg, Mississippi. To represent the North a few shingles from the log hut of Abraham Lincoln were exhibited. This reminds one of the beautiful play of the "Blue and the Gray."

Let us now pass through the center room. Over to the east part of the gallery, on the east wall, hangs the life-sized portrait of John the Baptist, painted by Murillo, 1613. In my judgment this was the finest painting I observed in the gallery. The thought came to me what must have been the joy it produced to Murillo 279 years ago. Fungi of all descriptions; also large collections of petrified wood. An elk horn imbedded in wood, from Baraboa; another from Black Earth, Dane Co., Wis. One chip of oak was at least two feet in diameter and the little oak very likely had grown in such a manner as to imbed the horns. A cut of a hickory tree six inches in diameter, with a board sticking in it caused by the great tornado in Wisconsin in 1865. A conch shell found one mile east of Lake Winnebago, 150 feet above the level and 10 feet below the surface. A small metal tripod from Italy; Venetian wine glasses; from Germany, (Mettlach), a beer mug pattern; from Egypt the hands of a mummy from Thebes.

I thought as I stood for a moment gazing at the withered hands of perhaps some queen, what jewels may have adorned thy fingers in thy youth, O queen! What king pressed thy hands and vowed to be true. But to-day thy earthly tabernacle is scattered to the four winds only to be gathered on that great day. My second thought was that it mattered very little what was done with the body after death, whether cremated, placed on exhibition or laid under the sod, so that our examples and influences were cast on the right side and for truth. In short, the immortality of the soul is more than all earthy gains and honors. The conquest of Mexico, 1519-21 was made impressive by a cannon which had been used as a hitching post for centuries in Tepie, having been carried there from Spain by the conqueror, Cortez. A Mexican's hat, weighing 1 lb., 10 ozs. It was a large, broad brimmed and high crowned hat, richly ornamented with a gold band. It was worth about $75. in our money. A small Aztec idol, very likely once worshiped in their temples or teocalli. The history of this tribe is very interesting to the student. A Tortilla stone, on which Indian corn is ground for pancakes. A large cutlass which had been worn in a belt by some Mexican. A relic from Andersonville Prison. It was a piece of looking glass placed in a small board frame, which had been cut out with a knife, and the piece of glass puttied in.

After dinner I started to visit the State University. The buildings are beautifully located on a cliff near a body of water. One large building is used exclusively for a chemical laboratory. A large number of students were constantly entering and leaving the main entrance. I did not remain here long but started towards the depot. On my way to the station a happy incident occurred which I shall never forget. Three little ill clad urchins were playing in front of a rickety dwelling. As I was passing by a little boy stopped me by asking, "Where is your home?"

My little boy, I live far from here.

"Well, I live there," pointing to the house.

I was about to pass on when he said "Give me a penny." I have only one and that has a hole in it, said I. " Well, give me that." I did so and they ran to the house filled with joy, where their mother met them and shared in their happiness. Verily, there was more joy in that family over the one cent, than ninety and nine dollars produced in my pocket.

Before arriving at the depot I passed by an old house which resembled a barn, and asked a gentleman what it was used for.

" There are a score of young ladies working there stripping tobacco."

I thought that was another way to elevate down trodden women, the future mothers of " Our grand and glorious Republic," to be shut up all day in a tobacco shop among green worms and tobacco smell, eking out their lives for a few cents, and under the very shadows of the capitol and universities.

The train has arrived and I am off for Milwaukee. On the right are people cutting ice with ice plows. There are also many sail sleds, which are used by some to take pleasure trips and others to convey the ice to the packing houses. The ground is becoming hilly and nice forests appear. Several inches of snow is still to be seen in the woods but the sun has thawn the greater portion of it to-day. The next is Sun Prairie which is a nice country town. The main part of the town is to the left. For many miles the pike and track run side by side. Many teams pass, barely noticing the trains as they pass them. There is some nice scenery along here. At Waterloo a large crowd of "drummers" got on. A white church edifice, to the right, is called St. Joseph. We move on to Waterloo Junction, a city of 10,000 inhabitants. They are commemorating St. Patrick's Day by wearing green ribbons. The college of the Sacret Heart and Catholic churches are here. A middle aged, jovial man and his wife got on and I asked him some questions regarding the city. "Yes;" says he, "I had almost forgotten, there are some breweries doing a big business, but please excuse me for giving any more information regarding breweries for my wife at my side might suspicion something." The sun is beginning to set and the heavens are putting on a strange appearance. In the distance the sun seems to be battling with a fog, but no: the moisture has turned into snow. I now begin to recognize the place and remember that last year I passed through here from Milwaukee to La Crosse, passing along the Wisconsin River, and noticed the Dalles, or canon, a deep cut some 8 miles long and 100 feet high. Some people were in boats on the river while many ladies and gentlemen were climbing the cliffs. Farther on, I remember, was a tunnel which made a very indelible impression on my mind.

We entered La Crosse as the evening shades were falling. The train is moving on towards Oconomowoc, a noted summer resort for the *elite* of Chicago, Milwaukee, New York, New Orleans and San Francisco. To-day it had a different appearance from what it had last Summer when I visited it. Then the waters were covered with boats containing merry fishing parties, now only a lovely winter scene is presented by the newly fallen snow. I also recognized the Armour Packing Co.'s ice houses, a long row of them containing millions of tons of ice. We now enter the metropolis of Wisconsin in the dusk of the evening. At the depot everything is hustling and every one is a hustler. It is a beautiful sight to behold the many head lights, and notice the escaping steam mingling with the frosty air. The switch lights are being carried to their places by men and women. The thought comes to me that in this age of invention this drudgery could be lessened by electricity, and the desired colors or signals produced by the operator simply turning a key located in the office.

After supper I started out for a stroll. The first attraction was a Salvation Army, singing as they were marching to their place of worship. After walking around a short time, I noticed a large crowd of people going to Davidson's theater and a larger crowd filing towards the Bijou. I was told that the play at the latter was the "Police Patrol," so I procured a ticket and entered. The architecture of the hall is beautiful and the place was well lighted by electricity. The principal feature of the play, which created a loud applause, was when the patrol alarm was sounded two white horses dashed out on the stage where they were harnessed in about eight seconds and in a few more seconds the driver and several policemen were on the wagon starting off on a gallop but stopped at the foot lights on a sudden, as the curtain fell.

In the morning I visited the docks. Here are scores of ships to be seen; many of them are being loaded with grain. A large City Hall is in progress in which all city offices will be located. The Schlitz Hotel is a large one and they are making preparations to increase its dimensions. As I had visited the main factories and beautiful parks last Summer, I concluded to spend the rest of my time at the Y. M. C. A. Hall, before leaving for Chicago. Before entering the main building I ate a very nice lunch, more to see what they had, and learned that their prices were very low.

I now enter the door to the main building. To the left is a reading room, in which is a well selected library. Here were many young men reading. To the right is an office where all the business is transacted. Nearing the center of the building we see stands on which may be played checkers, dominoes and all sorts of innocent games. In the room opposite the library is a piano which may be played by the visitors. In the rear is a gymnasium where all gymnastic sports are conducted under the critical eye of an instructor. There are bath rooms in connection with the building, and a large pool where the young men enjoy themselves by swimming. On the second floor is a lecture room. Before leaving I noticed an offering box in which I dropped a few cents to assist the carrying on of the good work.

The train having arrived, I was soon bounding along at a swift speed towards the Windy City. The sun is becoming warm and the lately fallen snow is fast disappearing. We are now at Two Mills, a small village, and I began to wonder why the place was called Two Mills. In the distance I beheld an English mill, sending up her curling smoke and steam, while farther on was a German mill, the wind turning the long, broad sails and these turning the mill stones. This is the same style mill used by the Dutch to-day farther up in the North-west, and as were also used by them in New York nearly three hundred years ago. I did not feel like a certain Knight, who, when he saw similar mills, drew his sword and began to fence with the revolving sails, but I concluded to let them stand as land marks, to show the progress of American intellect. I next notice an owl sitting on a tree.

A fire has burned the grass along the track and done some injury to the fence. The train is passing several small stations without stopping. The fruit vender is calling out "apples, oranges." Three squirrels are playing near a hickory tree. I was just in the act of calculating how many squirrels it would take to make a heap as large as an ordinary whale, when I beheld a good hay rake in a field which had been left out there by  some careless farmer. A nicely kept cemetery lies to the right. There are many log houses in this region, and before one of them is a a large apple orchard. A gentleman who was sitting near me noticed that I had made a memoranda of the cemetery, squirrels and apple trees.

"Where are you from?" he asked.

I said to him I am not an inhabitant of some distant planet, but have spent a part of my days in south-western Minnesota and her neighboring states. It is a rare thing to see a cemetery out there.

"Why, how is that?"

One reason is that tombstones are seldom

THE NORTH-WEST.

used and therefore, the cemeteries are not as visible as ours are in the East, where we have high monuments. Another reason is the people seldom die out here, for the air is very pure and healthy so that people who die in other regions, when brought here for interment, come to life; or, frequently when the proper authorities begin a search for the bodies, the tombs are empty.

"Do the authorities ever catch the body snatchers?"

Well, once they traced it to a medical college, but the students declared that as the winds were of sufficient force to move hay stacks from various parts of the meadows to the barns, it must be that the wind took a peculiar turn and scooped up the bodies and they were carried home on the wind.

"How do the live people manage from being blown away?"

Oh, that is explained easily: We do everything in companies. You remember the old maxim, "In union there is strength." Besides some of those people are larger and stronger than in the East. In fact, I have a man in my mind now, who was a butcher. When he had selected a nice, three-year-old heifer or steer, he would walk up to it, take the animal by the horns and throw it on the ground and hold it until the animal was strangled.

" How about the squirrels?"

There are none to be seen; formerly, a few flying squirrels were in this region but they improved the opportunity by taking advantage of the swift winds and flying off. As regards the apple trees, they do not grow there, for the winds in the Summer and the cold blizzards in Winter do not let them get a start, and it is a beautiful sight to see an orchard again.

The next I observe a small stump in the forks of a tree. The stump, I judge, being 15 feet from the ground. How it got there you may philosophize for yourselves. Three doves are venturing out from a barn yard to hail the oncoming Spring. A large pickle factory is passed by close to Forest Glenn. We are now nearing the City of Chicago. The blue smoke from the factories is seen in the distance. More sights are presenting themselves than can be observed creditably. Long rows of houses of the same style. Many factories are passed. The Pan Handle depot No. 1, follows in order.

We have now arrived at the grandest depot in the world. This is the second city in size in the United States and has a population of 1,100,000. Three hundred and seventy-five trains leave daily for various parts of the U. S., and passengers are constantly coming and going.

After dinner I called on the Commissioners of the Columbian Exposition and was kindly received by the gentlemen although they were very busy, at their main office near the center of the city. I asked them regarding keeping the grounds open on the Lord's day. Some thought it wise, others unwise. I remarked that if only those were allowed to enter on Sunday who were sober and could come out sober it might be all right, but the better way would be to close up every seventh day and attend services, if they had to erect a tabernacle where foreign talent might talk to their people, as well as home talent. Each factory, mill and shop employing help should give one holiday each month, so as to allow their employees to gather information without losing their positions. There is no need of walking to the World's Fair ground, unless one desires to do so, for street cars and conveyances are always in readiness. The location is on the Baltimore and Ohio Railroad, near Lake Michigan. Every effort is being put forth to make this the world's crowning feature. The grounds have a very large area and many of the beautiful buildings are nearing completion by the constant toil of thousands of employees.

One of the noted curiosities on the ground at

present is Lincoln's log cabin, which has been purchased by a number of gentlemen, who will place it under a tent, as a great many other things will be. A gentleman told me that his employer had $5,000 invested in the cabin, and thought the admittance fee would be $3. I said this looked like a money making scheme. "Well, we must all cut a sheaf while the harvest is on."

Amongst the noted features Austria will exhibit glass, porcelain, artistic iron and bronze. In the Woman's Building there will be a model hospital conducted entirely by Illinois women. In another part of the building will be found a historical collection of laces from Queen Marguerite, of Italy.

Denmark will exhibit a Danish dairy and show the most approved methods. A Pennsylvania iron company will exhibit a battle-ship shafting 125 feet long, also a full sized model 125-ton steam hammer, the largest in the world.

Each state in the Union will have a small lot with a building in which to exhibit that in which she excels : California may bring her gold and fruits ; North Dakota, her wheat; Nebraska, her corn ; Pennsylvania, her coal and iron ; Michigan, her lumber; Maine, her lobsters; Louisiana, her cotton ; but Ohio will bring a monument 30 feet high ; standing at its base will be such figures as Thurman, Garfield and Sherman, while on the apex stands the Roman matron, pointing down and seeming to say, I, Ohio, bring my men; these are my jewels.

I now passed back to the Board of Trade. I  remember of visiting the place last Summer when the wheat rose nearly 2 cents in a few hours. This was an exciting time. "Old Hutch" was out instructing his agents what to do. Many young striplings were gambling as heavily as the older ones.

To-day I visited the Rialto which also belongs to the Board of Trade. I had read a few days prior of Peter Maher, the pugilist, ascending and descending the stairs of Washington Monument, a height of 555 feet, on his way to the South to be whipped by Fitzsimmons, so I thought I would try and limber up by ascending the innumerable flights of the Rialto and descend them again in one heat. Instead of going South, however, I came very near going up to Minneapolis and have a round with Sullivan, for challenging me personally only a few days previous as he was passing through a town on the train, in southern Minnesota. The stakes were low and my trainers could not agree on the referee so we postponed it until he had taken a complete medical treatment at the Keeley Institute, after which he would undoubtedly kill himself like many other humbugged patients. Allow me to remark in this connection that the doctor, who has made such a great discovery, as he claims, and will not permit eminent physicians to examine it, but uses it for personal gains and aggrandizement, while his brethren are falling by the thousands every day, is a quack and a humbug in this dawning of the twentieth century.

Leaving the Rialto I visited the California Exposition of fruits and vegetables. After

asking permission of the manager to take a

few notes, which was gladly granted, and registering, I noticed, first, an enormous pumpkin, weighing 300 lbs.; the next article was a mangel wurtzel beet, weighing 70 lbs. and about 3 feet long; large ears of yellow and white corn; beautiful Burbank potatoes; a hill of sweet potatoes weighing 43 lbs; seedless lemons which grow by budding; specimens of olive wood; a eucalyptus tree, 4 years old and with a diameter of 6 in., raised at San Domingo, Cal.; yellow pine raised at Julian; an elderberry branch 1½ ft. in thickness; red cedar bark nearly 1 ft. thick; a second growth of barley since September, 1891; shaddocks 5 in. in diameter; beautiful slabs of marble; shells, nautilus, corals, etc; a collection exhibiting the different processes through which the silk passes—the worm, cocoon, moth and various manufactured fabrics, thus gaining an idea of the silk industry carried on in the Golden State; many cases of hard and soft shelled English walnuts; luscious peaches and pears; a specimen of Australian wheat, 6 ft. high; corn stalks 15 ft. high, so that a person would require a step ladder to husk it on the stalk; fine specimens of gold ore, which assayed a value of $708.92 per ton, which is exceptionally good as some in the Creed mines will not assay more than $20. per ton. By this we see that not everything that glitters is gold, also that the dross and gold are side by side and can only be separated by fire which is uncommonly hot. Next was a large piece of asphaltum, as black as jet; specimens of buckwheat, barley, wheat, hops, and beans in glass jars; ostrich plumes from Norwalk ostrich farm. Some of the feathers were black, others white. Do not look for more than one ostrich plume on your lady's Easter hat, unless she is a millionaire's daughter; licorice root, bent into the shape of a hoop; cotton—the plant, bloom, boll, photographs of picking, ginning and pressing; collections of choice figs, dates and peanuts; a nice collection of palm leaves and cat tail—reed mace, or typha; green olives and limes in glass cans.

I now leave the building and study the people for a time, principally to get some of their business ideas. I next visited an 18-story building after which many interesting places were more or less observed, principally the stock yards, Lincoln Park, boulevards, Palmer House, court house, custom house and post office, also several churches and school buildings. After supper I went to the depot and purchased a ticket for home and had my baggage checked. As the train did not leave until late in the evening I concluded to take another view of La Salle street, to study human nature under the electric lights, for one can find out more in an hour at night than in ten hours in the daytime. This statement will hold good not only with the aristocratic La Sallers but the world over. I passed mansion after mansion for miles. On returning I took the sidewalk instead of the car so that I could notice things more to my satisfaction. On arriving at Adams street, I started towards the depot. I had not quite gone a block when I I was politely asked by a powdered female to be her *chaperon*. This did not unnerve me for such occurrences are common not only in Chicago but in many wicked smaller cities and especially school towns. Instead of complying with her request I got on my dignity and offered to pay her hotel bill for a week if she would go to her room and not disgrace herself and her sex, and insult decent men who were attending to their business. She did not seem to be pleased with the proposition so we parted.

Just before I entered the train, I noticed about 75 foreigners with lunches, packs and valuables tied up in handkerchiefs enter a train for California. I approached one of the crowd and was told that they had come from all parts of Europe.

Our train whistles and we are traveling eastwards. Not much is seen until in the morning, when we were nearing Fort Wayne, Indiana. In the meantime, between a nap and a doze,

I was recalling first my experience as President of a Business College in the central part of the Hoosier state. How, Franklin like, I disposed of my valuable library by piece meal, so as to be able to obtain a loaf of bread or a lunch once a day and instead of sleeping in some unoccupied stair way, the floor of the college rooms served as a bed. I tried for a year to make an honest living in that vicinity by teaching day and evenings, without scarcely receiving any tuition which was due me for services. So finally concluded to join the staff of reporters and work on a daily paper but the preacher, with whom I had contracted, refused to pay the whole amount due me, "for" says he "we are at a great expense this year in building a church and I guess we must save up the money." I then followed stenography and type writing, but the lawyers were so dishonest that two were tried for forgery within a month. Another old gentleman, almost a septuagenarian, who had employed me to take a deposition, cheated me out of five dollars; but he ran to the end of the catalogue of sins in the decline of life by also committing forgery and was found guilty and sentenced to the penitentiary in the northern part of the state.

I finally worked my way in, as a book keeper and weigh master, in a canning factory and managed to eat two meals per day, and save a little money so that with it I might get out at least as respectable as I entered. But just as I thought I was getting along rather nicely the factory shut down for lack of fruits and vegetables to can. I now concluded to fall back to the humble but most honorable of all positions, that of laboring on the farm for a man, I will call him a man, although he had no more respect for God or man than one of those grunting porkers with bristles all over them; in fact if he had wallowed in the mud with the porker, and had the pig arisen on his hind legs and taken his stand aside of the human beast, I would have pronounced the pig, the man. I used to could stand to work 14 hours a day for six days out of the week, but to work 18 hours out of 24, (and the remaining six hours fighting fleas and bed-bugs) and seven days out of a week, harvesting on Sunday like on week days, was too much for my youthful training. So after pounding a few brains into the farmer's pate I started to visit a friend near Lake Michigan where I was treated like a King's son. This friend had also made a great discovery in the vicinity which I had just left. He found that he had lost several hundred dollars in the book business, so we could talk over our experiences. We struck up an acquaintance while in business and I considered that he was a faithful friend, at least according to immortal Shakespeare's views, which are regarded by me as being next to the Bible.

THE ORIGINAL PORTRAIT OF SHAKESPEARE.

> He that is thy friend indeed,
> He will help thee in thy need:
> If thou sorrow, he will weep;
> If thou wake, he can not sleep;
> Thus, of every grief in heart,
> He with thee doth bear a part.

While up here I visited the Hoosier slide, a ridge of sand on the lake shore as white as snow. The ridge is nearly 100 feet high and if a person has the "sand" to climb to the top, it will be an easy matter to descend. I ascended and descended without any difficulty, but a young couple met with quite a misfortune as they concluded to descend arm in arm; the lady lost her foothold, which caused the gentleman to lose confidence in himself, so for the next few moments, both were trying to gain their equilibrium but to no avail. Now they are falling; look out, they are coming faster and faster; every eye is turned upward; some are calling out to them to "hold on to the sand." This they strive to do. The danger is now past and some are laughing as the young couple reach the base all covered with sand, luckily not hurt, but wiser for the venture. This reminded me of woman's rights and suffrage. Some were laughing at the lady and said she had no business to go up there in the first place. But I thought she had an equal right to climb the ridge and get a view of the beautiful lake and scenery as any man or boy. A modest lady remarked: "If I was that lady I would not disgrace myself like that." That is very true, but by this bold lady's falls our modest sister may ascend and descend more easily. So with woman suffrage or female slavery.

It is an undisputed fact that God created all, male and female, equal—morally, mentally, and without any doubt physically, only in some things the females are more awkward than the males, for lack of practice. The same may be said of the males. It is also a known fact that all males unless insane, idiots, bribers, convicts, etc, after they have arrived at the legal age, are entitled to a vote. The females, therefore, being created the male's equal have also an equal right to vote. There are women who say, "Well I would not vote if I could." Of course we men admire their modesty and self-respect. But the simple fact that they have an opinion and express it as they do, would be expressed in the form of a ballot if the opportunity was presented them. Taking it for granted that these ladies would not vote, but only one out of a thousand, the way should be opened. Unless we men prove ourselves to be more than what our Creator declares us, we lower ourselves to the equal of slave holders, and should be dealt with accordingly.

I also visited the State Penitentiary where hundreds of criminals were at work, making barrels, boots and shoes, and knitting woolen goods. There were many undoubtedly in the prison who were innocent or had committed some deed while under the influence of liquor, but there were many others in whose faces were depicted the devil himself.

I then took a boat to Chicago and resolved to take Horace Greeley's advice and "Go West."

The train is now at Fort Wayne, the morning

is dawning and I see quite a city. It has a population of 35,000. The place was formerly a French trading post. The city has electric lights, street cars and many factories.

A wreck has just occurred near here, so our train will be delayed for a short time, until the track is cleared of the debris. The passengers on our train became frightened and excited, as the news of the wreck reached them. Fortunately no lives were lost. In life we know not when the Son of Man cometh, whether at midnight or at morn; it therefore, behooves us to be up and doing and be ready at all times.

We are now nearing the gas belt and a large derrick is seen in the distance. Passing through Van Wert, we see that she is a business city. The wheat in this region looks splendid. The next stop is at Delphos. Here is a fine Catholic church costing $60,000, and several high school buildings. I recall to mind that years ago, in this city, in my boyhood days, I wooed a school ma'am, and —did not lose, because I had never claimed her.

Innumerable derricks are appearing. We are nearing Lima and the place smells very strong of oil. Near the center of the town is a beautiful court house. There are many good hotels near the depot. At the depot I dropped a penny in the slot and discovered that I had gained 20 lbs. while in the West. Here also was a beautiful picture of Otter Tail range of the Rocky Mountains on the Canadian Pacific. I next take the train south, for Sidney. On the way I noticed large car shops and 333 oil tanks, each of which contains thousands of barrels of crude oil.

At Wapakoneta many passengers alight. Many nice churches and school buildings are seen but the saloons outnumber both. The wheat in this region is injured some by the March weather. We are now at Sidney. This place is having a slight boom. The castle on the cliff, near the depot, is a fine structure. The Sidney School Furniture Co. is located here. I noticed some of their seats in the "woolly West."

I now take a train east, for a short distance, and pass several small towns which are noted for nothing particularly, only as old land marks. The surface is now becoming rugged and the scenery beautiful. Some cliffs 150 feet high to the right while on the left flows a peaceful river. In this region are groves of sugar trees, with buckets hanging to them to catch the flowing sap. As we go on, the track makes a bend with the river, in the shape of a horse shoe, so that a person in the last coach can see the engine by looking out of the window. The surveyor must have had an eye to business, for this curve gives the engineer and ladies at least one chance to flirt with each other. I am next reminded by certain ancient land marks that the author has arrived

I had not been away quite as long as Rip Van Winkle, but many changes were noticeable. The thought that change is a natural law in the physical, moral and intellectual world made itself very impressive. Some of these which were observed by me will be portrayed from time to time. It was finally announced by the good people whose duty it is—or at least they make it their business—that the prodigal had returned. Then came a season of hand shaking which convinced me at least that I was welcome, providing I did not remain too long.

A change was observed in the social circle. I judge if there had been a Four Hundred Club in the village I would have been chosen in unanimously. A very striking difference was observed with the females. Perhaps because this is leap year. Some years ago, when I had less experience in the world and less renown, I admired a certain intelligent and refined lady in the village, but all efforts failed. What do I see to-day, since my Rip Van Winkle period or Robinson Crusoic adventure, but this very lady coming out, and also welcoming me home. Some boys who, when I left, were on the streets with torn knee breeches and mother earth on their bare feet, to-day are promenading the streets with the gentler sex, both having weak eyes, (at least wearing golden spectacles) and a "pug" led by the lady, while the gentleman sports a cane. Many of our most promising young men had chosen partners for life, while a number of good natured bachelors and maids were still in hope. I visited the cemeteries and observed that many of the young and aged had been lain in the silent tomb.

In a few days I visited a city farther east. On my way I passed by the log cabin in which I was born. I recalled my childhood days and one striking event which transpired. As we lived near the railroad I managed to crawl or walk close to the track and view the soldiers as they came home on flat cars. Of course I did not understand it then, but my perceptive faculties were aroused as they have been ever since. All that grieves me to-day is that this log hut has not gained sufficient renown to entitle it to a place in the World's Fair ground.

Farther on lies a beautiful lake, the waters of which resemble silver, and when the golden sun bathes herself in the water, as we boys used to do, it almost makes me wish I was a boy again. Arriving at the city I find that she is also on a boom. Many railroad shops are being built. Here I observed many financial changes: some have grown wealthy, others become poor.

A miserly old farmer for whom I worked through harvest, when a young man, at 20 cents a day, has failed and is now trying to make a living by day labor himself.

In the matrimonial line many changes were observed. In fact in our own family changes for the better, had occurred, which was almost considered an impossibility by me.

I next visited the poor house in the country and on my way passed the location where I had taught my first school. The house had been torn down and where the scholars used to sport was a flock of sheep lazily nipping the green grass. As I stood meditating over the past a neighbor came up to me and, after the ordinary greeting, remarked, "Well you are looking at your old school grounds, are you?"

Yes sir, and things have changed considerably around here.

"Yes, and there has been a great change with the scholars. Two brothers of one family are dead; one was drowned in the reservoir while on a fishing excursion, and he was to be married the next week. His brother, that stout, fleshy young man, you remember, died of consumption. Your largest scholar, who weighed almost again as much as you, has been married twice, his first wife not living long after their honey moon. Many of the girls are married also."

I now start on my way towards the Infirmary but really dreaded to go near, as I had almost become an inmate against my will, for some of the people thought I would never be able to make a living for myself. So to-day, I ventured in for the first time although having lived within three miles of the place for a score of years. The first inmate I met was an old acquaintance of mine who had become poor and sickly, so his well-to-do, haughty relations sent him here on the expense of the county, while his kind old wife had been sent out West to some of his friends to pine away the rest of her days. It almost caused my heart to cease beating to learn of his fate and remembering that he formerly liked sweets, I asked him if he would like a few pieces of candy. "Yes, give me a few pieces." I did so. Although I had faced many revolvers and death in more than one instance while in the West, I almost lost my nerve and turned away sick at heart, thinking how unreliable are even our nearest friends in time of need. The next gentleman was one with whom I used to labor on a farm. Well, my friend, said I, how are you? You remember we used to work together. " Yes, and I hope you will soon be with me here again." This remark was rather shocking to me but I took it the way he intended it. The usher then took me to see the idiots, decrepit, maimed, palsied and blind, all of which were pitiful specimens of humanity.

After staying all night at a friend's house in the neighborhood, I started in the morning to visit the Orphans' Home, not a great distance from the Infirmary. It was quite a treat to me to study the young child life and be permitted to visit their schools. Passing on westward, a short distance, I came to the place where my old school house used to stand, in which I first learned to read and spell (but not write). Nothing was left to mark the place only a few stones heaped up in a conical pile. The play ground was also altered; some of the trees back of which we children used to hide were chopped down. I remember my first day's experience at school; how I, a Saxon youth, pronounced the Pictorial Alphabet in my natural tongue although the lady teacher would have me to repeat the letters of the word after her, like a parrot, and then tell me to pronounce it, as she, but the Saxon word was uppermost and it would come first for I knew it was right according to the picture. Another mean trick I remember I was guilty of, was, that when the big girls would go to and from their recitations, I would try and embrace them,—a habit of which I have not yet entirely reformed. A few years later, when I was just learning to write and make figures, I had no slate, so concluded to write them on the wall, for I thought it was almost as black as the black board; but my gentleman teacher did not think so, and when I had done the deed he came up to me and took me by my waist collar, jerked me out of my seat and told me to sit under his high desk. Of course I did as he had commanded me, for fear of being killed. But I did not seem to mind it very long, at the time at least, for I kept on counting by touching my thumb, index, middle, ring and little fingers in their order on my forehead. Every time one of my fingers touched my forehead I would add one more to the sum. I can still see some of the larger scholars laughing at the teacher for his Yorkshire methods, and at himself, who was only a low and rotten round in the noble ladder of education.

Leaving this place I passed on a short distance farther and beheld another log hut in which I had been raised. In front of it stood a large spreading evergreen which had been planted by me when a child. This gave me courage and I resolved to

> Let the earth quake
> And the tree shake;
> But I will unfurl my colors,
> Though at times it proves dolerous.

I rested a few days at home then started to a classical city, some sixty miles distant, to visit the University of my youthful days. On my way out, I passed through a village where a farmer's daughter, with golden hair, and myself used to attend church and listen to the divine words which fell from the lips of the village preacher. I learned that she had married the gentleman whom she thought was a millionaire and poet, but she got sadly left on both, so they concluded to settle down and live with the old folks at home.

On arriving at the city in which the University is located I noticed that the place also had a steady, healthy growth. I remember that years ago when I alighted at the depot, there was an old, dilapidated structure there which could not hold rats. But what greets the travelers of to-day? A large fine building surrounded with green trees; also in place of water and mud the passengers are greeted by a newly erected monument which is an honor to any city. Scores of business houses and dwelings have been erected within the last decade. Formerly one school house accommodated the pupils of the city; to-day there are two high school buildings, one of them a new one costing $30,000 being in course of construction. In the line of churches, there is a noticeable effort to

build nice edifices. A fine brick structure is standing to-day on the ground where not many years ago, stood a small white frame building, with the plaster off of the walls and ceiling. In another part of the city the foundation is being laid for a second new church, which will be a large and fine structure. Still in another part of the city there are arrangements for the third new church. The changes and improvements in the University is likely the

topic of most interest, especially to the students. I now go back to my own recollections, when I entered, with satchel in hand and was called a "Moss back," "First termer," "Hay seed" or any of those genteel terms then used by the Juniors and some Seniors. Why? Simply because my pants were a little short or coat sleeves too long. But they are gone to fight the battles of life. Some are ministers of the Gospel, some are expounders of the law, others are becoming famous in medicine, music and literature, others have taken their places here, and some perhaps using the pet names their predecessors used. However this may be, I would gladly bear their chafings if we could only meet once more in society and reunion as of yore.

The President of the University, through his

untiring energy, has brought the school to such a high standard that she is even being recognized by our aristocratic Eastern colleges.

hundreds but to-day by the thousands. Three large buildings adorn the campus and a fourth one will soon be in progress. Three new departments have been added lately,—Pharmacy, Law and Military. It is a beautiful sight to witness hundreds of boys with their bright uniforms and glistening bayonets and swords, marching to the beating of the drum. The President has also built for himself a fine man-

sion instead of dwelling in the low "white house" Let me say before closing that the side walks which were formerly of boards and planks have been torn up (by the students, especially on Hollow Eve nights) and replaced by brick and stone walks. No more street lamps are used but the streets are now lighted by electricity and the students can no more hook grapes, take calves to chapel hall, take "aunt" from the museum and hang her on the telephone wires, go in squirt gun brigades, go to "Texas," tear up side walks, hook wood and a score of other deeds common to students, because the streets are as light as day and it would be an impossibility to hide from the piercing eyes of our beloved professors.

Many other instances might be cited and related to teach one to observe the changes which are constantly going on around us almost unnoticed. Suffice it to say in conclusion, that as everything organic is subject to change, so may your hearts change from the natural to the spiritual, that when life's difficulties are over we may all gather around the throne of the Lamb where changes and partings are no more through all the annals of eternity.

THE END.

www.ingramcontent.com/pod-product-compliance
Lightning Source LLC
Chambersburg PA
CBHW020859160426
43192CB00007B/989